Chartered Banker

STUDY TEXT

Contemporary Issues in Banking

In this 2014/15 edition

- A **user-friendly format** for easy navigation
- **Updated** on recent developments
- A **chapter review** at the end of each chapter
- A full **index**

Chartered Banker
Leading financial professionalism

BPP
LEARNING MEDIA

Published July 2014

ISBN 978 1 4727 0500 6

British Library Cataloguing-in-Publication Data
A catalogue record for this book
is available from the British Library

Published by

BPP Learning Media Ltd
BPP House, Aldine Place
London W12 8AA

www.bpp.com/learningmedia

Printed in the United Kingdom by Ricoh UK Limited

Unit 2
Wells Place
Merstham
RH1 3LG

Your learning materials, published by BPP Learning Media Ltd, are printed on paper sourced from sustainable, managed forests.

BPP
LEARNING MEDIA

CONTENTS

INTRODUCTION

The aim of this module is to provide an extensive, detailed and critical knowledge and understanding of contemporary issues in the banking industry and develop the practitioner's ability to make professional judgements and informed decisions in relevant work situations.

Learning Outcomes

The main learning outcomes associated with this module should enable you to:

- Examine the role of the bank as a financial intermediary and deposit creator
- Critically analyse economic theories, trends and the UK economic environment
- Examine the impact of monetary policy on banks, inflation, the housing market and the economy
- Critically review the involvement of banks in the international money, credit and bond markets
- Examine and analyse international factors impacting on banks
- Examine the ways in which public finance issues in the economy affect banks and critically analyse the implications of government shareholdings in banks
- Critically analyse the regulatory framework and the competitive environment in which banks operate
- Critically review the latest trends in innovation and technology in banking

Assessment structure

Your online extended response examination will be worth 70% of your overall result and your summative assignment will make up the remaining 30%.

Introduction to your study text

It is essential for a qualified banker to have a detailed and critical knowledge and understanding of contemporary issues within the banking industry. This Study Text aims to develop the practitioner's ability to make professional judgements and informed decisions about contemporary issues relevant to their work situations.

As a banker it is essential to understand the role of the financial intermediaries in an economy. A banker must also be able to critically analyse economic trends in the UK and global economies so that he or she can properly assess the likely demand for loans and other bank services. Economic knowledge as presented in this module will also assist in the proper assessment of loan risks, which is so essential in minimising losses and maintaining the financial soundness of banks.

A key factor in such knowledge is a proper understanding of monetary policy and its impact on banks, the economy and the housing market which this module seeks to address. In addition, a banker must have a thorough knowledge of bank operations in the global financial markets and the risks associated with such activities. All aspects of securitisation and globalisation must be understood along with the creation of the EU single banking market and its likely impact on competition in the banking sector.

A banker must also understand the major public finance issues being debated in most countries and how these impact on national economies and banks. In many countries the recent financial crisis and ongoing recession has forced governments to acquire stakes in banks in order to maintain financial stability. The Eurozone crisis has also added to the problems of bankers as regards actual and potential debt write-offs which have resulted in demands for banks to have additional capital and liquidity adequacy ratios against their assets.

Against such financial maelstrom and international bank regulatory agencies are new rules and guidelines for balance sheet management, corporate governance and competition. As this Study Text will explore, the latter has the potential for a major restructuring of the banking sectors in many countries and it is against such a background that banks have to decide their operational and marketing/product strategies in the future. To this potential mix is added the impact of new technology in the delivery of bank services and internal management of banks.

It is against the above financial and economic background that this Study Text seeks to explain and critically analyse major contemporary issues in UK and global banking.

chapter 1

FINANCIAL ASSETS, LIABILITIES AND INTERMEDIARIES

Contents

Learning outcomes

On completion of this chapter, you should be able to:

- Explain the concept of the national balance sheet and sector surpluses and deficits
- Explain the domestic recycling of funds and the creation of direct and indirect financial claims
- Evaluate the role of financial intermediaries in the economy and how banks serve savers' and borrowers' needs
- Comment on the personal sector balance sheet and explain fluctuations in the personal sector savings ratio
- Examine the role of the bank as a deposit creator and analyse the concept of the bank deposit multiplier

Introduction

Understanding the concepts of the national balance sheet and financial wealth are essential in order to appreciate the role of financial intermediaries. By a process of aggregation, maturity and risk transformations, these institutions create primary and secondary financial claims which suit the asset and liability portfolio requirements of all economic agents in a country. The personal sector, by its steady accumulation of financial wealth via unspent income, encourages financial institutions, companies and the government to adapt and provide a wide range of financial products. A modern economy requires a flexible and adaptable financial system.

In this chapter, we will consider some key aspects of financial wealth and intermediation:

- Sector surpluses and deficits
- Domestic recycling of funds
- Financial claim classification
- The personal sector savings ratio/net worth
- Personal financial products
- Deposit creation and its limitations

These aspects and others will be considered in the context of each economy's need for the optimum utilisation of the nation's savings resources in order to maximise economic welfare.

To aid in the understanding of such concepts as financial wealth and intermediation, we will examine a country's financial system. The first step is to consider the national balance sheet.

1 The national balance sheet

This lists all the assets and liabilities (the claims held and claims due) on a particular date for an economy.

**National Balance Sheet of Utopia (£billion)
as at 31 December 20XX**

A	Physical Assets			150
B	Financial Assets			
	1	Money	20	
	2	Loans	50	
	3	Shares	90	
	4	Life Policies	20	180
				330
C	Financial Liabilities			
	1	Money	20	
	2	Loans	50	
	3	Shares	90	
	4	Life Policies	20	– 180
D	Net Worth (A + B – C)			150

The balance sheet for the hypothetical country of Utopia emphasises the fact that physical assets, such as land, buildings, roads and machinery, represent the real wealth of a nation. These physical (or capital) assets play a major role in the generation of income within an economy by assisting in the production of goods and services. Note that financial assets and liabilities cancel one another out, thus making net worth equal to the value of physical assets.

The reason for this equality of values arises from the fact that a financial claim is simultaneously an asset to one economic unit and a liability to another, linking the two economic units. For example, bank notes held by an individual are an asset to the holder, whereas to the issuing authority – the central bank – they are a liability.

A bank deposit is an asset to the individual as the holder of the claim, but it appears as a liability in the bank's balance sheet. The same applies if you hold shares or make a loan to a friend or relative. The financial system is in effect a superstructure built on the real wealth of a nation – its physical assets.

An economy can be divided into various sectors and the net worth of each one – physical *plus* financial assets *minus* financial liabilities – can be ascertained:

- The public sector incorporates central and regional governments along with various state agencies, such as Scottish Water

- The industrial/commercial sector constitutes private corporations which produce the goods and services in a market economy

- In most economies the bulk of net worth is attributable to the personal sector, i.e. private individuals

For the sake of simplicity, the overseas sector is omitted. Thus we are examining a closed or domestic economy.

QUICK QUESTION

Why do you think private individuals hold most net worth?

Write your answer here before reading on.

The net worth of any sector in an economy can be calculated by adding up all the assets it holds *minus* financial liabilities to other sectors. The net worth of the personal sector of Utopia will be equal to the physical assets *plus* financial assets held, *less* any financial liabilities it has to other sectors.

The personal sector may be in the following position:

	£billion
Physical Assets	50
Financial Assets	100
	150
Less Financial Liabilities	– 60
	90

QUICK QUESTION

What is the net worth of the other sectors in Utopia?

Write your answer here before reading on.

Thus, the personal sector of Utopia has a net worth of £90 billion. You would generally expect the personal sector of an economy to be in a net credit position. Equally you would expect the public sector to be in a net deficit position because its financial liabilities to other sectors in most cases will far exceed its financial assets. The public sector has a tendency to spend more than it receives in tax receipts and thus is forced to borrow from other sectors of the economy, thereby creating and adding to the national debt.

QUESTION TIME 1

Ascertain the net worth of the following sectors in Utopia from the figures below and the National Balance Sheet data as at 31 December 2013.

£ billions	Industrial/Com. Sector	Public Sector	Personal Sector	Total
Physical Assets	25	?	50	?
Financial Assets	?	30	100	?
Financial Liabilities	25	– ?	– 60	– ?
Net Worth	?	?	90	150

Write your answer here then check with the answer at the back of the book.

Let us now take our analysis one step further to see how financial claims are created and the role played by financial institutions in this process.

2 Funds flow analysis

This measures financial transactions between various economic sectors in a country. A sector has a financial surplus if total receipts exceed total expenditure for a particular time period, and *vice versa* for a financial deficit. The key problem of finance arises because saving does not equal investment for each economic sector.

The surplus sector must acquire or purchase financial claims (assets), and/or pay off outstanding debts, i.e. claims held against it. Obviously, a deficit necessitates the opposite course of action – the issue of financial claims (debt) or a run-down in financial assets held. The act of borrowing and lending gives rise to financial claims. The holders (savers) of assets and suppliers (borrowers) of claims create a financial market in some form.

One of the main aims of all financial institutions, including banks, is to channel funds from financial surplus to financial deficit units in an economy. Banks borrow money (surplus) from the personal sector, i.e. take deposits, not to finance their own deficits, but in order to finance other sectors' deficits. This is sometimes referred to as the domestic recycling of funds within an economy.

A simplified annual funds flow statement is shown below.

Utopia Sector Analysis (£billion)

	Public Sector	Industrial and Commercial Sector	Personal Sector	Total
Year 1	– 10	– 2	+ 12	0
Year 2	– 8	+ 2	+ 6	0
Year 3	– 6	+ 1	+ 5	0

The figures indicate that the financial system enables the personal sector to put its financial surplus at the disposal of the other two sectors in the form of increased holdings of bank notes, bank deposits and shares. Some people save for short periods of time, perhaps receiving their income at the beginning of the month and spending it later. Others may save for longer periods in order to make an expensive purchase or investment. In some cases, it might be a matter of principle to save income in excess of needs.

Some of the surplus might pass through financial institutions, such as banks and insurance companies, rather than holding direct claims, such as share or loan certificates, on other sectors. Note that the figures zero out in each year as financial assets and liabilities are opposite sides in the creation of a financial claim.

In most economies, the public sector is invariably a net borrower due to its expenditure being in excess of its tax revenues, so it is obliged to issue financial claims, i.e. bank notes, government stock, national savings certificates, premium bonds. Such action increases a country's national debt. On the other hand, the private sector in most economies is nearly always a net lender via increased holdings of various types of financial assets.

QUICK QUESTION

Why do economic sectors have deficits and surpluses?

Write your answer here before reading on.

3 Financial claims

A financial claim arises whenever an act of lending or borrowing takes place in an economy. Financial institutions and markets channel funds from surplus sectors to deficit sectors. Financial intermediaries borrow, not to finance their own deficits, but the deficits of other units.

Most financial claims (excluding bank notes) carry an obligation on the issuer to make periodic income payments and to redeem (repay) the claim at a stated value to the holder. This might be fixed, such as a loan with a fixed interest rate and repayment date, or variable, such as dividends on ordinary share capital (common stock), the latter in most cases not being subject to repayment by the issuer, as the corporation will be in existence indefinitely; for example, BP plc or General Motors.

In most cases, if the holder of shares wishes to recover the money balance paid to the company which issued the shares, then the shares must be sold in a secondary market, i.e. a stock exchange, to some other party. The existence of such a market guarantees the reversibility of such a claim, but not the disposal price or value. The ability to dispose of financial assets enables the holders of such claims to indulge in asset switching to suit their own needs, such as selling shares to increase bank deposit balances.

Every financial claim has some degree of risk attached to it. With a bank deposit it is relatively easy for the holder to recover the money balance, risk is low and so also is the rate of return. The greater the risk, as with ordinary shares, the higher the rate of return expected by the holders of such claims. Financial claims are generally classified according to the degree of liquidity associated with each claim – notes, bank deposits, government bonds, shares, life policies, etc (highly liquid to least liquid).

For the personal sector, most financial assets thus provide some form of return, are marketable and can be converted into cash at minimal expense and inconvenience. It is the convertibility aspect that attracts people to hold a certain proportion of their wealth in financial assets. The alternative is the ownership of physical assets – land, houses, cars, etc – which might appreciate or depreciate in value, incur maintenance costs and require to be insured against theft or accidents. The disposal of physical assets sometimes might involve considerable expense and inconvenience, such as legal documentation associated with land and property transactions.

Each year in the UK, the personal sector increases its holdings of various financial assets – bank notes/deposits, national savings certificates and shares – and also contributes to life assurance policies and pension schemes, which in turn acquire financial assets, such as domestic and overseas bonds and shares.

QUICK QUESTION

What do you understand by the term financial intermediation?

Write your answer here then check with the answer at the back of the book.

4 Financial intermediaries

Financial intermediaries, such as banks and insurance companies, acquire direct or primary claims on deficit units and issue to the public their own secondary claims to finance such acquisitions. Let us now consider claims on a bank and how they are created.

BANK INTERMEDIATION

Personal Sector Bal Sheet (£m)		Albion Bank Bal Sheet (£m)		British Petroleum Plc Bal Sheet (£m)	
Liability	*Asset*	*Liability*	*Asset*	*Liability*	*Asset*
Capital or Net Worth	Albion Bank A/C	Personal Sector Deposits	Loan to BP	Albion Bank Loan	North Sea Oil Field
100	100	100	100	100	100

Issue   Issue

Indirect/Secondary Claim   Direct Claim/Primary Claim

In this simplistic illustration of the creation of financial claims, the personal sector has an asset in the form of a secondary claim issued by Albion Bank. Albion Bank has both a financial asset and a liability. Its financial asset is the direct primary claim it holds on British Petroleum while its financial liability is the secondary claim issued to the personal sector.

In most cases, secondary claims are more attractive to surplus units (the personal sector) than direct claims on deficit units because they can get their money back when it suits them – they have liquidity. Intermediation costs (financial institutions' operating costs) must be paid from the bank's margin between borrowing (deposit) and lending interest rates. Such costs are reduced by the scale of their operations.

Most financial intermediaries are thus involved in a process known as asset or maturity transformation, whereby deposits generally have a shorter term than have their loans – banks borrow short and lend long.

The liabilities of financial institutions are quite willingly accepted as financial assets by their holders, i.e. bank depositors and insurance policy holders. Because the holder has faith in the financial intermediary, risk is reduced and convenience achieved, as some financial return on savings is derived without the need to investigate the ultimate borrower. A financial intermediary also helps by taking everyone's savings and aggregating them to make a large pool from which large borrowings or investments can be made. If the intermediary, in aggregate, has large inflows of savings deposited for varying periods of time, it can mismatch the maturities of its liabilities (what it owes to savers) and its assets (what it is owed by borrowers). This means that it can use short term deposits of savings to finance long term borrowings because it is confident that, throughout the life of long term borrowings, short term deposits will normally always be coming in to finance them.

Let us now consider claims on an insurance fund (pension fund, unit trust).

INSURANCE FUND INTERMEDIATION

Personal sector balance sheet (£m)		Happy Widows Assurance Fund balance sheet (£m)		Kinross Oil Plc balance sheet (£m)	
Liability	*Asset*	*Liability*	*Asset*	*Liability*	*Asset*
Net Worth 200	Life policies pension 200	Life policy pension claims 200	Kinross Oil Plc 200	Ordinary shares 200	Gas field 200
		Indirect or secondary claim	shares Direct or primary claim		

In this situation the Happy Widows Assurance Fund has life policy claims of £200m outstanding. It holds £200m worth of ordinary shares issued by Kinross Oil plc which has used the money raised to invest in a gas pipeline. The share holding is a direct claim held by the Happy Widows. These shares can be converted into cash by selling them on the stock exchange to other investors.

Financial intermediaries thus provide a link between lenders and borrowers and channel funds from those with a financial surplus to those in deficit. Many savers will save only relatively small amounts for varying time periods and do not know how to get in contact with potential borrowers. Even if they did, they would not want to incur the risk of non-repayment. Such people make use of the services of financial intermediaries – e.g. banks, insurance companies, pension funds. There may be more than one link in a chain which channels funds through a number of financial intermediaries before the link between the ultimate lender and ultimate borrower is complete, such as the inter-bank market.

QUICK QUESTION

Without financial intermediaries, how could individuals spend more than their income?

Write your answer here before reading on.

The ability to borrow allows some groups to spend more than their income by tapping the surplus financial funds of other groups. Without this facility, people could only spend in excess of their income by:

- Running down money balances previously acquired
- Selling off physical and financial assets for money

Competition, particularly between deposit takers, i.e. banks and non-banks, is based primarily on deposit and loan interest rate differentials, access to funds, the size of the branch network, opening hours and provision of ancillary services. However, despite any differences, all financial intermediaries must manage their balance sheets to ensure that no fundamental mismatch arises between deposits and loans as regards maturity and interest cost. Sufficient liquid assets must be held at all times to meet sudden fund withdrawals by customers.

5 Other aspects of financial intermediation

Financial intermediaries minimise the risk of loss by the lender(s) through the potential default by the ultimate borrower by spreading the risks through making a large number of loans (or investments) of varying degrees of risk, return and maturity. The institution reduces its own risk and thereby that of the ultimate lender(s). At the same time, the capital and reserves of the institution should enable it to sustain any possible loan or investment losses, without jeopardising the financial position of the lender(s).

As already mentioned, lenders prefer short term claims, whereas borrowers prefer long term funds. Financial intermediaries resolve this problem by maturity transformation – borrowing short and lending long. Institutions can do this because the sheer scale of their operations ensures that daily withdrawals will be matched by new deposits. Experience also enables institutions to deal with seasonal flows and make adjustments in returns to deal with the ebb and flow of funds made available by lenders and requested by borrowers.

Financial intermediaries also minimise borrowers' risks. Direct sources of funds might not be available when required. Through their deals with many lenders, intermediaries should be in a position to supply funds under agreed terms at most times. Their diversified asset portfolios enable them to consider a wide range of lending options which will meet the needs of most borrowers.

Finally, financial intermediaries, due to the scale and diversification of their lending operations, can minimise their transaction costs, which should benefit borrowers via lower interest charges or cheaper equity.

Summarising this section on financial intermediation, financial institutions – e.g. banks, building societies, insurance companies:

- Provide financial services at a low cost
- Assist lenders and borrowers
- Encourage saving and investment, thereby
- Promoting a higher rate of economic growth (in most countries)

In a narrower context, banks act to the advantage of both savers and borrowers while hopefully making a profit for their owners, the shareholders.

Savers' interests

- To find a safe place for savings with the minimum risk of default
- To have ready access to their money should they need it earlier than expected
- To diversify savings as a way of further reducing risk and spreading liquidity
- To maximise the return on savings while minimising the cost of finding a reliable borrower

Borrowers' interests

- To find an institution willing to make a loan

- To obtain a mortgage or loan at minimum cost

- To obtain the necessary funds at the time required

- To have the use of the funds for the period required without the risk of demands for early repayment

QUICK QUESTION

Distinguish between physical assets and financial assets.

Write your answer here before reading on.

6 Financial assets and physical assets

So far we have considered how certain sectors will have financial surpluses while other sectors will have financial deficits. We have seen how financial claims arise and that financial intermediaries exist to channel funds from surplus units in the economy to deficit units. Before moving on to study financial institutions and the products they offer, we will clarify the differences between financial and physical assets and why sectors hold each kind of asset.

A financial asset should provide some form of return, either as a dividend or an interest payment. To count as a financial asset, a claim must not be conditional. A life assurance policy is a financial asset because the money is paid either on death or on survival at a specified date. A fire insurance policy is not a financial asset because it is only paid in the event of a fire actually occurring, as covered by the policy. In most cases, a financial asset is marketable and can be converted into cash at minimal expense. It is this convertibility aspect which attracts people to hold financial assets, such as bank deposits, building society share and deposit accounts, certificates of deposit, government stock and ordinary shares.

Most people hold financial assets – bank notes and coins, bank account balances – to meet their immediate needs for the purchase of essential consumer goods. The more liquid the financial asset, the lower the rate of return; in the case of bank notes, no return is paid.

The degree of risk associated with each financial claim varies. As a result, the return is related to this risk factor. If a company goes into liquidation, then its financial claims – ordinary share certificates held by the owners – become virtually worthless. No secondary market exists for worthless shares. Even if a company is basically sound, the value of its financial claims – ordinary shares and debenture stock – will fluctuate in the stock market according to demand and supply, which is influenced by a large range of diverse financial/economic factors operating in the economy. As opposed to a company's shares, building society share accounts offer a lower return in exchange for less risk and greater stability of value.

Physical assets, such as houses, cars and computers, can yield utility in the form of pleasure from use. In some cases, physical assets can generate a financial return if rented or hired out to other parties. Some physical assets can be sold in a secondary market. Unfortunately, their second-hand value may be well below the initial purchase price, mainly due to depreciation (cars, washing machines, computers, etc). Other physical assets, such as houses and land, tend to appreciate in value over time.

It is not so easy to convert physical assets into financial claims (bank deposit or cash), as is the case with shares. To sell a house, a market must exist for it, and considerable expense is associated with the legal fees incurred in buying or selling property. Unlike a share certificate or a government stock certificate, a property is not transportable and must be sold in a limited local property market.

Physical assets also require to be insured against risks such as theft or fire. Total loss resulting from physical asset ownership is less likely than is the case with shares owned in a liquidated company, although ultimately a car or a washing machine will cease to function and thus be worthless.

It is for these reasons that individuals prefer to hold a combination of physical and financial assets. Some physical assets, such as a house, may retain their value in real terms during times of inflation, whereas financial assets, such as bank notes and deposits, become worth less in real terms, yet the latter must be held to retain maximum convertibility and be capable of meeting daily transactions.

QUESTION TIME 2

List and explain the reasons why people save money.

Write your answer here then check with the answer at the back of the book.

7 Development of a financial system

From a general perspective, a financial system develops in the following stages.

1   The initial stage is the introduction of money to replace a barter system.

2   The next major development is that of borrowing between the various economic sectors and units. Units with a net financial deficit may borrow from units with a surplus. Generally the deficit unit issues an interest-bearing financial claim, such as a loan or bond. These claims become financial assets for the surplus units. This stage has been initiated in many countries by governments having to borrow funds to meet expenditures in excess of tax revenues.

3   Deficit units and surplus units must now be brought together so that financial claims may be created which may also be traded, leading to the development of stock markets.

4   This leads to the development of financial intermediaries who are able to provide maximum liquidity to surplus units, such as bank deposits, while also providing loans and longer term finance to other units. They are therefore meeting the needs of both surplus and deficit units while making profits for themselves by lending at a higher rate of interest than they pay the surplus units.

5   Also a system develops whereby, through the purchase of equity securities, surplus units may gain control of a public company without having to manage it. Such equity securities are bought and sold on the stock exchange.

6   The final stage of development relates to asset switchers and liabilities switchers. The former are those units that change the composition of their portfolios by selling one claim and buying others with the proceeds. Financial intermediaries may fall into this category. The switching of assets in this manner indicates a high degree of substitutability between financial assets. Governments are the major liability switchers through the various methods used to obtain finance; for example, national savings certificates, premium bonds, Treasury bills or bonds.

QUICK QUESTION

What are portfolio institutions?

Write your answer here before reading on.

Personal sector balance sheet

Utopia Personal Sector
Balance Sheet as at 31 December 2013 (£billions)

Tangible Assets				
	Residential Buildings		40	
	Vehicles & Other Assets		<u>10</u>	50
Financial Assets				
	Notes/Coin	10		
	Bank Deposits	25		
	National Savings	5		
	Government Stock	5		
	Company Securities	10		
	Life Assurance	20		
	Pension Funds	<u>25</u>	100	
Less Financial Liabilities				
	Bank Loans	10		
	Mortgages	40		
	Other	10	– 60	40
Net Worth				<u><u>90</u></u>

(*Note:* The statistics in this and subsequent tables do **not** require to be memorised for exam purposes.)

The personal sector's balance sheet indicates that residential buildings are the main asset held by people in Utopia. It also accounts for the main financial liability, i.e. house loans, in the balance sheet. Among the financial assets, although bank deposits are important, company securities, life assurance and pension funds combined are more than double in value. Bank loans and other credit are associated with purchases of consumer durables, e.g. cars, TVs, washing machines. As to be expected, the personal sector has an overall net worth position. The above hypothetical balance sheet is representative of most western countries, subject to national differences in the relative importance of particular physical and financial assets.

If Utopian net personal sector wealth was £80 billion at the end of the previous year, this would imply a £10 billion or $12^{1}/_{2}$% increase over the course of one financial year. However, it might be that most of this increase was due to inflation in the housing market rather than an increase in the value of financial assets and/or decline in financial liabilities. In other words, the increase in net worth is not due to increased savings out of disposable income.

In 2010, the UK's net worth was estimated at £6.6 trillion. Housing was the most valuable asset with a value of about £4 trillion, or 60% of the country's net worth. Civil engineering works, e.g. roads, railways, accounted for around £700 billion, or 10% of net worth.

QUESTION TIME 3

Compare and contrast the main attributes of physical and financial assets using a Ford Focus and National Savings Certificates as examples.

Write your answer here then check with the answer at the back of the book.

QUICK QUESTION

Why do people switch their holdings of financial assets?

Write your answer here before reading on.

People switch their holdings of financial assets for a number of reasons. It might be to enhance the potential yield or reduce the element of risk associated with holding a particular financial asset. Liquidity preference might be another determining factor. A person may prefer to hold a savings account balance rather than a long term bond. Shares might be sold so as to raise cash for some specific purpose, such as house improvements or a world tour.

8 Personal sector savings ratio

This ratio examines the relationship between personal sector savings and total personal disposable income, i.e. gross income *minus* compulsory deductions such as tax.

The formula for calculating this ratio is:

$$\text{Saving ratio} = \frac{\text{Personal savings}}{\underset{\left(\text{Salaries} - \text{Tax and NIC deductions}\right)}{\text{Total personal disposable income}}} \times 100$$

In most economies, figures for the personal sector's savings ratio are available in the form of a time series. As to be expected, it is not a constant ratio; instead, it fluctuates over time due to underlying economic and social developments in a country.

Figures for the hypothetical state of Utopia are:

Personal sector: Savings ratio

Year 1	5.7
Year 3	8.6
Year 5	12.5
Year 7	10.1
Year 9	9.0

In the UK, the main use of available funds each year has been the ongoing high level of investment in life assurance and pension funds. The personal sector appears to prefer secondary claims via institutions, such as life companies, to primary claims in the securities markets. This is the continuation of a long term trend that has not been reversed in spite of government privatisation of formerly publicly-owned companies by means of share issues.

Personal financial products

We will now switch our attention briefly to the main personal financial products made available by financial institutions, companies and the government.

In the UK, over 50% of financial assets held by the personal sector are in the form of financial claims issued by life assurance companies and pension funds. It is, therefore, hardly surprising that banks and building societies have increased their presence in this financial product sector.

The main financial liability consists of home loans provided by banks and building societies. Bank lending is also an important source of finance to a large number of households. Most of these funds are used to finance consumer expenditure, such as the purchase of cars.

Banks and building societies are the main providers of liquid assets to the UK private sector, so that competition between them for market share of current, deposit and investment accounts, etc, is likely to remain intense in the future.

Personal sector holdings of UK company securities as financial assets have declined in recent years due to the increased volatility in share prices. This encouraged the personal sector to reduce the number of shares held and to invest the sale proceeds in various low-risk savings facilities.

 **QUESTION TIME 4**

(a) Suggest possible reasons for the rise in Utopia's personal sector's savings ratio from Year 1 to Year 5 and its subsequent decline by Year 9.

(b) Comment on the UK's personal savings ratio rising from about 2% in 2005 to 6% in 2010.

Write your answer here then check with the answer at the back of the book.

9 Bank deposit creation and money supply

The Bank of England can try to influence the level of economic activity and inflation rate by altering interest rates or money supply. Such a strategy is known as monetary policy, which requires the Bank to control bank deposit growth in the economy by the various means at its disposal.

9.1 Bank deposit creation

Money deposited by customers

Bank deposits can be used for the discharge of debts by means of a cheque. Bank deposits are thus regarded as much a part of the country's money supply as bank notes and coins. Bank deposits are initially created by customers depositing cash in a bank which opens an account in their name and credits it with the deposit amount. In simple balance sheet terms, the bank has an asset, cash, and a liability, a deposit claim against it, for an equal amount.

Loans granted by banks to customers

Bank money can come into existence not only because people deposit money with a bank, but also because banks grant loans to their customers. In such cases, it would be inconvenient if the bank had to pay out cash. Instead, the bank adds the sum to the account of the customer to whom the money is being advanced.

The customer can now draw, in cash or by cheque, not only that part of their account which constitutes money actually paid in by them, but also that part of the account which has been advanced by the bank. The granting of the loan has increased the spending power of the customer – money has been created.

Overdraft facilities granted to customers

Overdraft facilities also create money as soon as the customer draws cheques against these facilities, because the cheques must be paid into a bank account somewhere, thus raising the total level of bank deposits.

In the case of a customer loan, the creation of money takes place when the granting bank credits its customer. In the case of an overdraft, money is created as soon as the cheques drawn against the overdraft facilities are paid in, either to the same bank or to other banks. This is the explanation of the sentence, often used to explain credit/deposit creation: every advance creates a deposit.

These three methods of deposit creation are now illustrated by a simple balance sheet in a single bank economy.

Albion Bank

	Liabilities		Assets	
1	Bank Deposits	1,000	Cash	1,000
2	Bank Deposits	2,000	Cash	1,000
		2,000	Loan	1,000
3	Bank Deposits	3,000		2,000
			Cash	1,000
			Loan	1,000
			Overdraft	1,000
		3,000		3,000

QUICK QUESTION

How might a bank's ability to create credit be limited?

Write your answer here before reading on.

9.2 Limitations on bank deposit creation

The creation of bank deposits (money) by the banking system, which generates more profits for individual banks, is subject to important limitations. Briefly, these are:

- **Sufficient demand for loans and overdrafts, i.e. advances**

  Demand must come from safe, creditworthy customers with the ability to repay advances. In the early 1990s one of the factors contributing to the depth and length of the economic recession was the lack of the right sort of bank borrowers. Banks could not find safe borrowers offering adequate collateral security.

- **The liquid asset position of banks must be adequate**

  UK banks must maintain adequate liquid assets – e.g. cash, bills, money at call – to meet repayment of deposits. Through money/securities market operations, the Bank of England can adjust the amount of liquid assets available to the UK banking system.

- **The need for banks to keep in line**

  No individual bank can afford to expand its lending faster than the other banks in the system unless it can attract extra deposits from the public. In a five bank system, a bank with only 20% of the market would expect 80% of the loans it made to be re-deposited with other banks and this would require a transfer of cash from it to other banks. There would, of course, be transfers back as the loans created by competitors were re-deposited with it. If the bank created loans at a faster rate than its competitors, there would be an imbalance in these transfers and a loss of cash liquidity for the bank.

- **The total amount of cash in the country**

  The amount of cash available to the banks to support the expansion of their deposits will be influenced partly by the total amount of cash in the country – the more cash there is, the more cash is likely to be left with the banks. The desire of the public to hold money in the form of cash, rather than as bank deposits, will also influence deposit creation in the economy.

9.3 Deposit creation and liquid assets

- **The effect of granting a loan**

  A loan given by a bank to one of its customers will raise advances on the assets side and deposits on the liabilities side of the bank's balance sheet. As the bank's liquid assets are unaltered while its deposits (and assets) have risen, its overall liquidity will decline. Each bank must maintain a

BPP
LEARNING MEDIA

minimum level of liquidity to retain customer (and shareholder) confidence. If liquidity falls below this level, the bank cannot grant further loans (or any form of advances) to customers.

- **The effect of granting overdraft facilities**

    Overdraft facilities granted by a bank to one of its customers will have a similar effect on the bank's liquid assets as soon as the facility is drawn upon. If the customer draws cash, the bank's holding of cash falls and advances rise as the customer's cheques are debited to their new overdraft account; the composition of the asset side on the bank's balance sheet thus alters.

If cheques are drawn to pay bills and these are paid in at other banks and then presented for payment through the clearing system, the bank granting the overdraft must transfer part of its Bank of England operational balance to the presenting bankers in settlement. These cheques are then debited again to the customer's new overdraft account.

In both cases, the bank's cash has fallen, while advances have risen. As deposits have remained unchanged (assuming recipients of such funds have accounts with other banks), the proportion of liquid assets may fall below the required minimum.

Summary

Individual commercial banks create money when they grant loans and overdraft facilities to their customers. This power is conditioned by several factors, such as the monetary authorities' requirements concerning minimum liquid assets and their policy concerning bank lending, the maintenance of liquid assets by the banks themselves and their willingness to undertake bank lending.

10 Liquidity ratio

Let us now assume that banks have to maintain a 10% liquidity ratio against deposits. Liquid assets might be comprised of:

- Cash
- Bank of England operational balances
- Money at call
- Bills discounted
- Government stock (gilts), with less than a year to maturity

At this stage it will be obvious to you that the requirement to maintain a 10% liquidity ratio against deposits reduces a bank's ability to make loans (advances), as such action increases its deposits, against which must be held the 10% liquidity ratio. If we further assume that the Bank of England controls the supply of liquid assets included in the ratio, then control of the growth of advances, deposits and money supply is within its grasp. As we shall see (in Chapter 3), control of the supply of liquid assets is one of the main levers of monetary control used in the UK economy.

Simplified Illustration of One Commercial Bank Economy

Stage I   **B/S (£)**

			Liquid Assets	100
Deposits	500		Advances	400
	500			500

$$\text{Liquidity ratio: } \frac{\text{Liquid assets}}{\text{Deposits}} \times 100$$

$$\frac{100}{500} \times 100 = 20\%$$

Stage II

		B/S (£)		
Deposits	700		Liquid assets	100
			Advances	600
	700			700

Liquidity ratio: 14.3%

Stage III

		B/S (£)		
Deposits	1000		Liquid Assets	100
			Advances	900
	1000			1000

Liquidity ratio: 10%

Note: Assume

1 A single bank system, i.e. there is only one bank in the country

2 No leakages, i.e. bank deposits are generally acceptable as a means of payment, and people who receive bank deposits are perfectly happy to hold them and do not attempt to turn them into cash

3 A fixed supply of liquid assets in the country of £100

4 A constant level of demand for cash

5 The bank decides to keep a 10% liquidity ratio

In the three stages, you can see how a commercial bank could expand its advances from £400 to £900, and still comply with the 10% liquidity ratio. It is also apparent that, if the Bank of England reduced the supply of liquid assets, then the volume of advances, deposits and thus money supply, would decline in the economy.

Stage IV

		B/S (£)		
Deposits	980		Liquid assets	80
			Advances	900
	980			980

Liquidity ratio: 8.2%

Stage V

		B/S (£)		
Deposits	800		Liquid assets	80
			Advances	720
	800			800

In Stage IV, the Bank of England, via money market operations, reduces the liquidity ratio to 8.2%. In order to restore the ratio to 10%, the total level of advances is reduced by £180 to £720, with a consequential contraction in deposits of £180.

11 Credit creation in a multi-bank system

Credit creation in a multi-bank system (an economy in which there is a number of banks) is more complicated, but the final result is much the same. In a multi-bank system, when bank X makes a loan (and creates a matching deposit) there is no guarantee that a cheque drawn on that deposit will be re-deposited with bank X. It may go to bank Y or bank Z which would mean that bank X would need to transfer funds to bank Y or bank Z and so would lose cash.

If banks Y and Z are also making loans, there is likely to be transfer of funds in the opposite direction. These movements tend to cancel each other out, so that in practice the banks are only concerned with settling their net imbalances.

In a multi-bank system:

- There is need for a clearing house to resolve inter-bank differences. Each clearing bank keeps a current account at the central bank (the Bank of England). Payments and settlements of imbalances are made from one bank to another by cheques drawn on their operational accounts at the central bank.

- Banks are aware that the creation of loans can lead to a leakage or loss of cash.

12 Bank deposit multiplier

In the example, liquid assets of £100 were used to support total bank deposits of £1,000 (Stage III). This is known as the bank deposit multiplier process. The original deposit of liquid assets has been multiplied to total deposits of £1,000 via the granting of £900 of advances. The multiplier value in this case is 10.

Assume the government needs to borrow £200, which it partly finances by issuing more notes or cheques drawn on its account at the Bank of England. If the notes and cheques are deposited by private sector recipients in our bank, both assets and liabilities increase by £200 from the Stage V position.

Stage VI

		B/S (£)		
Deposits	1,000		Liquid assets	280
			Advances	720
	1,000			1,000

Liquidity ratio: 28%

The bank is now in a position to expand its advances/deposits as it has adequate liquid assets.

Stage VII

		B/S (£)		
Deposits	2,800		Liquid assets	280
			Advances	2,520
	2,800			2,800

Liquidity ratio: 10%

The bank has expanded its advances by £1,800. Deposits have also grown by a similar amount. The liquidity ratio is at the statutory minimum of 10%.

This relationship can be shown by the equation:

$$\text{Bank deposit multiplier} = \frac{1}{\text{Liquidity ratio}} = \frac{1}{1/10} = 10$$

Or, to put it another way, the multiplier is the reciprocal of the liquidity ratio. So a liquidity ratio of 10% (or $1/10$) gives a bank deposit multiplier of 10. A 20% ratio would give a multiplier of 5.

The amount of bank deposit multiplier process depends on the amount of cash (notes) and Bank of England cheques deposited and retained at the bank. It also depends on the multiplier's value.

QUICK QUESTION

What determines how much cash is deposited with banks?

Write your answer here before reading on.

The amount of cash deposited with the bank will be influenced by the total amount of cash available and the public's desire to hold cash. Some Bank of England cheques may be deposited in the bank and then be transferred back to the Bank if private individuals decide to purchase national savings certificates or gilts.

The amount of cash deposited with banks will be influenced by:

- The total amount of cash available
- The public's desire to hold cash
- The public's trust in the banking system

The bank deposit multiplier concept helps us to understand the deposit creation process in a country's banking system. However, cash and deposits can leak out of the banking system due to changes in people's liquidity preference or by transfers to the government. As a result, the deposit multiplier is less stable and predictable in the real world than textbook examples imply.

QUESTION TIME 5

(a) Calculate the bank deposit multiplier for liquidity ratios of 12.5%, 6% and 4%.

(b) Taking Stage VI balance sheet, draft a new Stage VII balance sheet assuming a liquidity ratio of 4%.

Write your answer here then check with the answer at the back of the book.

KEY WORDS

Key words in this chapter are given below. There is space to write your own revision notes and to add any other words or phrases that you want to remember.

- Physical assets

- Capital assets

- Real wealth

- Net worth

- Public sector

- Industrial/commercial sector

- Personal sector

- Financial surplus

- Financial deficit

- Domestic recycling of funds

- Rate of return

- Liquidity asset or maturity transformation

- Intermediation

- Financial claims

- Personal sector savings ratio

- Bank deposit creation

- Bank deposit multiplier

R E V I E W

The main learning points introduced in this chapter are summarised below.

Go through them and check back to the learning outcomes at the beginning of the chapter. Only move on when you are happy that you fully understand each point.

- The concept of the national balance sheet enabled us to distinguish between physical assets and financial assets and introduced the concept of net worth for economic sectors.

- The role of financial intermediaries includes aggregation, maturity and risk transformations. The ultimate importance of intermediation is to ensure that savings are put to good use, that investment and output are increased and that the total utility and welfare of society are greater than they otherwise would be.

- We examined the personal sector in order to identify the main sources and uses of funds, along with the computation of its overall net worth.

- We considered deposit creation by banks and the limitations imposed on this activity by balance sheet constraints and the maintenance of an adequate liquidity ratio. We also examined the bank deposit multiplier.

In summary, we looked at:

- The national balance sheet and funds flow analysis
- The main aspects of financial intermediation
- Differences between physical and financial assets
- The main items included in the personal sector's balance sheet
- The personal sector savings ratio
- The bank deposit creation and its control
- The bank deposit multiplier